Old Doune and Deanston

by Bernard Byrom

This 1913 photograph was taken in Moray Public Park, situated off Moray Street, Doune. The occasion was the 21st birthday, or 'coming of age', of Lord Doune, the Earl of Moray's eldest son. The local celebrations were immense; Doune castle was illuminated, the adults celebrated in various ways, and the children paraded from Main Street to the castle waving Union Jacks. A floral arch was erected across Main Street at Braehead, on the bend by the Roman Catholic church, carrying the slogan 'Long Live Lord Doune', and afterwards everyone spent the afternoon enjoying a variety of entertainments in Moray Park which included the Punch and Judy show pictured here. As part of the celebrations 21 lime trees were planted around the perimeter of the park; ninety-five years later they have all survived.

This intriguing photograph is believed to have been taken in Doune around 1904. It appears to show a chemist or druggist making up a prescription and in those days there certainly was such a person recorded in the official directory for Doune. His name was Walter Thomson and his shop was on the corner of Main Street and The Cross, in the premises now occupied by Wood'n'Tots.

First published in the United Kingdom, 2009,
by Stenlake Publishing Ltd.
www.stenlake.co.uk
ISBN 978 1 84033 462 3

Acknowledgements

The author wishes to thank the following for their assistance during his research for this book: Nigel Bishop, Lynn Bowser, Robin Chapman Campbell, Susanne Rae and Ian Ross.

Further Reading

The books listed below were used by the author during his research. None of them is available from Stenlake Publishing. Those interested in finding out more are advised to contact their local bookshop or reference library.

Moray S. Mackay, *Doune Historical Notes*, 1953 (republished 2003).

Moray S. Mackay, *The Castle of Doune*, 2008.

A.F. and S. McKenzie, *Doune Postcards from the Past*, 2001.

Archie McKerracher, *Perthshire in History and Legend*, 2000.

Karen Ross, *Around Doune and Deanston*.

(All the above books can be obtained from the Information and Development Centre at 52 Main Street, Doune, FK16 6BW.)

The Statistical Account of Scotland, 1791–1799.

The New Statistical Account of Scotland, 1845.

Leslie's Directories, 1897–1940.

Young's Illustrated Guide to Doune and Neighbourhood, 1898.

Introduction

The ancient burgh of Doune lies four miles west of Dunblane and eight miles south-east of Callander. It is the capital of Menteith, more correctly spelt Monteith, which means the mouth of the River Teith and was once one of the great earldoms and provinces of ancient Scotland. The town stands where the Ardoch Burn comes down from the northern heights to join the Teith, which rises several miles further west in Loch Lubnaig and the Trossachs. To the north of the town are the Braes of Doune, which stretch up to the heather hills of Ben Vorlich and the Forest of Glenartney.

The main part of the old town, which roughly runs from west to east, is built on either side of Balkerach Street which leads via The Cross into Main Street and out towards Dunblane. Several old streets such as George Street, Graham Street, Moray Street, King Street and Queen Street extend from either side of The Cross and Main Street.

In 1611 the village was granted the status of a Burgh of Barony by King James VI and this gave the Earl of Moray the right to erect a cross in the market place to mark the place where the formal business of the burgh had to be conducted. A subsequent Act of the Scottish Parliament in the reign of King Charles I required 'all proclamations and executions formerly used at Tapielaw of Down to be made at the Mercat Cross of Down'. It is nowadays thought that this cross may have stood further down Main Street in front of the position of the first parish church, built in 1746, which was further back from the road than the present building.

The original cross was probably only a pillar set in a large stone but the present-day Mercat Cross is a pillar ten feet high that stands on a base of six square steps. Its capital is formed by two sundials on the south and west sides and by two shields. The shield on the eastern face displays the Moray arms and the one on the northern face displays those of the house of Argyll because the fifth Earl of Moray married a daughter of the ninth Earl of Argyll. The figure surmounting the shaft is said to represent the Lion of Scotland. A mercat cross was a symbol of a burgh's right to trade. Markets and fairs were held up to six times a year between the 1600s and the 1800s but by the late nineteenth century, as the great cattle fairs faded away, they were replaced by smaller markets.

Doune is situated in the ecclesiastical parish of Kilmadock whose original parish church was a long, narrow and plain structure situated on the northern bank of the Teith two miles west of the town. The building eventually became unfit for worship and the minutes of the Kirk Session of 10 July 1743 record the decision that 'future meetings for divine worship will be held at Doune Castle until such time as the intended kirk at Doune is fit for our reception.' This new Kilmadock church in Main Street was finally completed in 1746 but only lasted for 74 years before another new church with seating for 1,121 worshippers was built in front of it in 1820 (it was completed in 1824). At one time, in addition to the parish church, there were no fewer than six other churches in the little town – these were the Free, the United Presbyterian, the Wesleyan, the Auld Lichts, the Roman Catholic and the Episcopalian.

One of the local lads who made good was Alexander Ferguson. He was a poor local boy who was born in a little house in Graham Street and who went to Edinburgh in search of work. He became adept at manufacturing sweets and it was he who invented Edinburgh Rock. His sweets became famous worldwide and made him a fortune. When he retired back to Doune he purchased most of what is now Graham Street, which became known colloquially as Sweetie Lane. He died in 1871 in the house he had built for himself nearby at Glenardoch and which is nowadays a bed-and-breakfast establishment.

Doune had a postal service as far back as August 1793 when a runner was employed between Callander and Dunblane every Sunday, Tuesday and Friday. Collections were made from Edinburgh at 9 p.m. on Mondays, Thursdays and Saturdays and the post arrived at Doune early the following morning. Postage of a letter cost 3d. (1.25 pence). Old maps show that the post office appears to have been originally situated in Balkerach Street at what is now No. 41A near the present-day bus stop. There were also weekly carrier services to Stirling, Dunblane, Callander and sometimes to Kippen. By 1844 the postal service had increased to a daily mail-gig between Callander and Stirling and a stagecoach which ran between those places daily in summer and twice weekly in winter, whilst the carrier service had expanded to two carriers twice-weekly to Stirling. With the coming of the railway the service improved still further: by 1900 letters were received at

Doune Post Office at midnight, 7 a.m. and 5.31 p.m. and letters were despatched at 7.45 a.m., 3.50 p.m. and 7.10 p.m. Compare that with today's collection and delivery times!

The railway came to Doune in 1858, but the town didn't have a regular bus service until 1928 when an Edinburgh–Callander service was operated by Alexander's Bluebird buses. Nowadays the traveller can go no further east than Stirling without changing buses, whilst the railway closed in 1965.

Doune was also renowned for its manufacture of high-quality pistols. The earliest manufacturer was Thomas Caddell, who was born in nearby Muthill and who began making pistols in Doune sometime around 1646. He was soon joined in the same trade by other craftsmen and their elaborately ornamented and highly accurate pistols became world famous. Caddell's factory, now an office, still stands behind No. 35 Main Street. Highlanders in particular were fond of sporting them, but this market declined following the 1745 Jacobite rebellion when the Proscription Act was passed banning the wearing of Highland dress. However, pistol manufacture continued in the town until around 1800 when advances in precision-engineering tools finally resulted in their replacement by cheaper ones that were usually made in Birmingham. However, in recognition of its skill in this art, the burgh sign shows two pairs of crossed pistols on either side of the Mercat Cross. Today a genuine Doune pistol fetches several thousands pounds at auction. Sporrans were also made in the town, but as these were also banned by the Proscription Act a different kind of manufacture came to replace them – cotton manufacturing at nearby Deanston.

Dan Kennedy was a slater by trade but is best remembered as a local poet. Many of his poems were on local topics and a good example appears on page 16 he lived in Doune at Glengarry Cottage, which is No. 68 Main Street.

This photograph dates from around 1910 and looks eastward from the Cross towards the beginning of Main Street. The premises on the right belonged to Parlane McFarlane, painter and confectioner, whilst the newsagents next to it belonged to William Allan. Then come the premises of Andrew Sinton, shoemaker, and James Murray, fruiterer. The tall building next door was a bank. In 1840 the Glasgow Union Banking Company opened a branch in what is now the Woodside Pharmacy at the Cross. In 1843 it changed its name to the Union Bank of Scotland and in 1875 it moved into this grander building across the road. In 1955 its name changed again, this time to the Bank of Scotland. The branch eventually closed down and the building is now the premises of Webb & Wallace, accountants. However, the bank's initials 'UBS' can still be seen carved in stone above the first floor windows. Banks seem to have had a hard time in Doune. In 1855 the Royal Bank of Scotland opened a branch in Sweetie Lane (now Graham Street) and later moved into premises in Main Street (where the Village Store is today) but it closed down in 1904. It is still possible to make out its name on the lintel of its former entrance in Graham Street. The Commercial Bank of Scotland's branch had an even shorter existence, opening in 1922 and closing in 1941. There are nowadays no banks at all in the town, only a cash machine in Main Street. The shop on the left is Duncan Young's newsagent's shop.

Another early twentieth-century view of the shops at the Cross with Main Street beyond. The first building on the right is Mrs Sarah Wynter's draper's shop, nowadays Jennifer's Hand-Made Chocolates, Flowers and Gifts. The next two buildings were Cochrane's baker's and MacFarlane's confectioner's shops; nowadays these are respectively Clandon House and Woodlane Clothing and Gifts. Beyond them, the former shops of Andrew Sinton and James Murray have recently been refurbished into a shoe shop. Mary Macfarlane's fuiterer's shop on the left of the picture is nowadays the Woodside Pharmacy, which is currently (2009) planning to extend into the former premises of the newsagent and bookseller's shop pictured next door. Note the water hand-pump at the base of the cross, which indicates that the town did not yet have a supply of piped mains water when the photograph was taken, and the stone posts at the four corners of the plinth. These were erected in the late nineteenth century to protect the cross from traffic damage but twentieth-century motor traffic proved too much for them. They were eventually removed after being badly damaged but were restored during conservation work on the cross in 2004. Also in the picture is a small weighbridge that was positioned in the roadway just in front of the cross. Many people regarded it as an eyesore and there were few regrets when it was removed some years ago.

By the time this 1930s photograph was taken Young's newsagent's had become Mackenzie's. The shop is currently closed (its last occupant was A.C. Rennie) and will re-open as an extension to the chemist's shop next door, which was at one time Mary Macfarlane's fruiterers. Beyond the two doors to its right, the shop with the rounded windows (which are unchanged today) was once the premises of John Thompson, chemist and druggist, and is now Wood'n'Tots, then comes a private house with a rounded doorway named Rob Roy House. The two shops beyond it have nowadays been converted into the Doune Library and the Gingham House Coffee Shop and Bistro. Parlane Macfarlane's shop is still there on the extreme right of the picture but there are various changes since the previous photograph. The water pump and protective stones have gone from around the cross, the church clock face is now the more conventional white colour and the Balhaldie Inn beyond it has significantly gained in height with the addition of four flats above it.

This photograph was taken further down the street from the last one; on the extreme right is the Commercial Hotel, nowadays the premises of Harvey mapmakers. This is followed by two blocks of houses and then a larger building which is now a Costcutter shop. On the left are two businesses, one of which appears to be a barber's shop; nowadays, these are private houses, numbered 15 and 17. Next to them is Mrs Helen Forster's Temperance Hotel, now the Highland Hotel, and these are followed by a row of houses as far as Moray Street which runs off to the left just before the fine Kilmadock Parish Church. Its construction began in 1820 and while it was opened for worship in 1822, it wasn't completed until two years later. This picture shows that its clock originally had a black face but around 1930 this was replaced by the more usual white face by Messrs Briggs & Ferrier; in 1970 it was converted to electric operation. The arms of the Earl of Moray adorn the tower above the main entrance archway. In the 1950s one of the spires was hit by lightning and crashed to the ground; after that the remaining spires were removed for reasons of safety. The church was built with seating for 1,121 worshipers but could hold 1,400; however, dwindling congregations in recent years have led to its closure and in 2008 it was sold for private development. The first building beyond the church is the Balhaldie Inn, which dates from 1732 but there may have been a hostelry in this location long before that time. In 1910 the inn was enlarged by the building of four flats above it and this is how it appears in later photographs. The inn is now closed and as of 2009 has been refurbished as a retail outlet, but the flats are still there above it.

The far end of Main Street, at the east of the town, is known as Braehead. It was often photographed a century ago and was described on picture postcards as 'A Bit of Bonnie Doune' (1906) and 'A Pretty Corner of Doune' (1907). This 1928 scene is largely unchanged today except for more foliage on one house and none at all on the others. The cottage on the left is now named Darroch Cottage. The old set of double steps leading down to the road, seen jutting out into the roadway in the picture, have been removed, presumably as they were a safety hazard to modern motorists. Queen Street runs off to the left just beyond the large house facing the camera, which was built in 1835 as the malt barn and is still known by that name. The gates on the right lead up to St Fillan & Alphonsus Roman Catholic Church. It was built in 1875 to hold about 300 people, the cost of erection being borne by Mrs Campbell of Inverardoch. Before it was built the Catholics of Doune had to walk the eight miles to Stirling to hear Mass; it is said that they used to walk there barefoot with their boots slung round their necks and only put them on when they got to Stirling, which says a lot about the roads of the time! The house and shop on the right, No. 76, belonged to Robert Ainslie, Doune's well-known glass and china merchant and general dealer.

Below left: On the old Dunblane road, past Glenardoch House and across the Ardoch Burn via the Auld Brig o' Doune, is a private drive leading up to Old Newton, the oldest surviving building in the area. It is an L-shaped harled fortalice and is unusual in having a rounded gable instead of the usual square shape. At one time it was the home of a branch of the Edmonstone of Duntreath family who were the hereditary captains of Doune castle. Legend has it that Bonnie Prince Charlie called here in 1745 on his way south to the ford at Frew and that he took a glass of wine offered to him by the daughters of the house who asked to kiss his hand, a request he was pleased to grant. This encouraged their young cousin, Miss Clementina Edmonstone of Cambuswallace, to ask him for a kiss on the lips; apparently the athletic young prince obliged her without dismounting from his horse. There are many versions of this story, some placing the event at Cambuswallace, but as the Prince was on his way from Dunblane to Stirling via the ford at Frew the author believes that Newton is the more likely place. Sir Walter Scott also stayed here and it is thought that he wrote some of his poem 'The Lady of the Lake' during his visit.

Above: On the opposite side of the road to Old Newton is Castle Farm. The original farmhouse was situated much nearer to the castle but as part of the latter's restoration project in the early 1880s it was demolished and the handsome building shown here, with its crow-stepped gables and crest above the windows, was erected on this site below Newton and appears virtually unchanged today.

It's only a short walk back across the Auld Brig to the castle of Doune which stands on a narrow peninsula of land between the River Teith and its tributary, the Ardoch Burn. The castle became a royal residence in the fifteenth century and was frequently visited by the Stuart kings who enjoyed the hunting nearby. It was also used as a dower house by three queens: Mary in 1449, Margaret of Denmark in 1469 and Margaret Tudor in 1503. Since 1580 it has been owned by the Earls of Moray who derive from it their title of Lord Doune. It was the one-time home of James Stewart, who was murdered at Donibristle in Fife by the Earl of Huntly in 1592 and who is celebrated in the well-known Scottish lament 'The Bonnie Earl of Moray'. The castle also features in Sir Walter Scott's novel Waverley and, nearer to the present day, was the setting of several scenes in the films *Monty Python and the Holy Grail* and *Ivanhoe*. During the Jacobite rising of 1715 the castle was a rebels' garrison and in 1745 was visited by Bonnie Prince Charlie who used it to house up to 150 prisoners. The tree in the foreground was known as the Gallows Tree, its purpose being evident from its name. It was blown down in a gale in 1878 at an advanced age and its timber was used to manufacture several pieces of furniture for the Baron's Hall in the castle. The castle seems to have been built at different periods of time and was never completely finished. Its restoration began in 1883 by order of the fourteenth Earl of Moray and to mark its completion a concert was given in the castle on 28 August 1886.

Most of the present castle was built by Robert, first Duke of Albany, who was the brother of King Robert III of Scotland and who had married the heiress Countess of Menteith. Both he and his son Murdoch, the second duke, were in turn appointed Regents of Scotland during young King James I's enforced exile in England. But the king deeply distrusted them and when he eventually returned from exile in 1424 he showed his gratitude to Murdoch for governing the country in his absence by chopping off his head! In 1570 the ownership of the castle passed to Sir James Stewart, who was the first Lord Doune. Subsequent marriages brought the family the earldom of Moray and the castle has belonged to the Earls of Moray ever since. After the Jacobite rebellion of 1745 the castle fell out of use and by 1800 it was in a ruinous condition. In 1883 the fourteenth earl undertook its restoration largely to its present condition and further repairs were made in 1970. In 1984 the twentieth earl placed the castle in the care of the nation on a 999-year lease and it is now looked after by Historic Scotland.

The castle consists of two huge and lofty keeps that are linked by a lower range of buildings, all surrounding a central courtyard. The north side on the right of the picture contains the notable Great Hall which has a fireplace in the centre of its floor and forms one side of the quadrangular court whilst the other three sides are enclosed by a curtain wall that is 40 feet high, 8 feet thick and topped by a parapet and walkway. The Gatehouse keep, which is on the extreme right in the picture, is the older and higher of the two keeps.

Left: The principal entrance into the castle was through a huge wooden door, behind which was an iron-grated door (known as a 'yett') which led into a 46-feet-long passage through the Gatehouse Tower. Part of the way along the passage was a second door heavily constructed of oak and studded thickly with iron nails and at the far end there was another yett. In between the gates was a long slit in the passage roof through which the defenders, in the event of attackers having breached the outer door and yett, could fire down on them. The fortifications were completed by a portcullis between the outer door and yett which could be lowered from a room above the doorway. The wooden door in the picture is a modern replacement and the floor is now cobbled but the yett itself is original and still in position although the inner gates have gone.

Above: The well in the courtyard, once the castle's only source of fresh water, is around 20 metres deep and during restoration work in 1883 an old wooden windlass was recovered from its depths. This was reinstated at the top of the well and lasted for many more years until, on one cold night during the Second World War, two soldiers who were stationed at the castle chopped it up to use as firewood. The Gatehouse keep is to the right of the well, showing the passageway from the outer gate into the courtyard. The roughness of the ground underfoot contrasts markedly with today's neatly cut lawn in the courtyard.

The Baron's Hall, also known as the Duke's Hall, is situated in the Gatehouse Tower adjacent to the Great Hall and is one of the most important rooms in the castle. It is on the first floor above the gateway passage and is reached from the courtyard by an enclosed stone stairway. The walls are lined with wood panelling, the floor is tiled with red and white tiles, and the plaque above the minstrels' gallery at the far end commemorates the room's restoration. The inscription, around the Moray coat of arms in its centre, reads, 'Restored by George Philip Stuart, 14th Earl of Moray, 1883'. The furniture in the room was carved from the remains of the Gallows Tree after it was blown down in 1878. On the right, the large window looks out onto the approach road to the castle and in its sill is a timber flap which, when lifted, enabled the defenders of the castle to hurl missiles down onto any attackers who had managed to get into the passageway below.

This photograph from the battlements above the Duchess's Hall dates from around 1903 and shows a rural scene that is almost unrecognisable today. The cottage in the foreground was the home of the Castle Keeper; it is still there but now serves as the public toilets for visitors to the castle. Doune Primary School now occupies centre-stage in the field beyond the cottage with the Castle Hill housing estate occupying the remaining space between the school and Main Street, which runs across the picture in the background. In recent years the outline of a Roman camp has been discovered in the field near the school; it has been dated to around AD 800 and probably included a hospital. Two church buildings can be seen in the photograph, apart from the parish church in the centre. The large gable end of St Fillan's Roman Catholic Church is prominent to the right whilst the spire of the West Free Church is plainly visible on the extreme left. This church became redundant after the rapprochement between the Established Church and the Free Church in 1929 which resulted in the East Church in Main Street becoming the parish church. In 1961 the west church's spire was removed and the building was tastefully converted into two private houses. Nowadays the view from the same spot is very restricted; only the parish church and a few buildings either side of it can be seen above the foliage and the modern housing developments.

Apart from nowadays having a slate roof and the open porch enclosed, the appearance of the former Castle Keeper's cottage is virtually unchanged. Towards the end of the nineteenth century the Castle Keeper was a man named Macdonald who was nicknamed 'Dancie' because of his sideline as a dancing master. At the other end of the path that led along the riverbank to the Bridge of Teith there lived the local gamekeeper, Duncan Dow, who was a terror to the local children. The two men conspired together to prevent the public from using the path by fixing padlocks to the gates at either end but the locals were having none of it. Every time the padlocks were fixed they were forced open and were found next day in the river. In the end the path was left open and the conflict was celebrated in the above verse by the local poet, Dan Kennedy. The hill from the Bridge of Teith up to the town is still known as 'Dan Doo's Brae'.

Back in the village centre, this photograph looks from Main Street towards Ainslie Brothers' butchers' shop at the Cross with their van standing outside; Balkerach Street runs off to the right and George Street to the left. Ainslie's is nowadays Charlotte Grace Bridal Collections and the taller building next to it is Kesara Therapies. The other buildings to its left are still private houses. George Street used to be known as Pudden Wynd because of the number of butcher's shops in it that sold black and white puddings. It later became known as Chapel Street because of its two churches (Episcopal and Wesleyan) and was finally renamed George Street after the Rev. George Mackay who financed the building of a block of houses at the top of the hill.

Balkerach Street runs westwards from the Mercat Cross to the main Callander Road. In the mid nineteenth century a good part of Doune was made up of 'Wee Thack Hooses'; these covered most of Balkerach Street, the west side of Queen Street and the east end of Main Street, most of Moray Street and some of George Street. As the century progressed most of these were re-roofed in slate and the last thatched houses in the town were the ones pictured here in 1923. In 1848/49 there was a bad cholera outbreak caused by the unclean water at the well, which was situated just out of the picture to the right, close by the modern day bus shelter. The view down the street is very similar today, except that the thatched cottages and the taller block beyond it are no longer there and have been replaced by two more modern bungalows, the one further away being named 'Dalavich'.

An atmospheric photograph of part of Balkerach Street in 1910, showing the opposite end from the previous picture. The low wall is still there, belonging to No. 12 and nowadays with newer and lower railings. The nearest house with the bootscraper by the doorway is No. 16, nowadays called 'Ormonde House'. The house next door is unnamed and those beyond have been replaced by the two bungalows mentioned on the previous page, the nearer one being 'Dalavich'. The two little boys are obviously dressed up for a special occasion; they may have been taking part in a parade or maybe it was just their 'Sunday best' for going to the kirk.

The Dunblane, Doune and Callander Railway was opened to passenger traffic on 1 July 1858 as a single line branch with a station at Doune; however, the volume of tourist traffic by the turn of the century led to the line being doubled in 1902 when the new station, pictured here, was built, opening on 5 June that year. The Dunblane, Doune and Callander Railway was taken over by the Scottish Central Railway on 31 July 1865 and by the Caledonian Railway on the following day. After the line was extended to Oban in July 1880 most services went through to that town but there were also additional local services between Callander and Stirling. In 1923 the Caledonian became part of the London, Midland and Scottish Railway and upon nationalisation in 1948 it became part of the Scottish Region of British Railways who, in the late 1950s, ran the very popular Six Lochs Land Cruise on Sundays using diesel multiple units. Dwindling rail traffic in the 1960s caused by the growth of private motoring led to a decision to close the railway to passenger traffic between Crianlarich and Dunblane from 1 November 1965, but this was pre-empted by a rock fall in Glen Ogle on 25 September which closed that section of the line permanently. Freight services were withdrawn from Doune in June 1965 and the station was demolished in 1968. The modern housing development at Station Wynd was built on the site of the station; the start of Pistolmakers Row is effectively the position of the station entrance.

The Woodside Hotel has old origins; around 1800 it was recorded as being a small wayside inn that was owned by a Mrs Somerville who had a sign above the door in the shape of a white swan. The green in front of the hotel used to be common ground that was once a location for summer cattle markets and was later a drying or bleaching green which extended along the roadside of what is nowadays George Street towards the Draigen Burn. The 1898 guide to Doune records that from time to time 'Cheap Johns' and travelling shows used to carry on a brisk trade on the open ground in front of the hotel. It was also a favourite place for holding tent and open-air religious services; until such time as they were able to build their own churches, it was here that the breakaway United Presbyterian Church congregation, which was formed near Thornhill in 1740, held its earlier services, as did the Free Church after the Disruption of 1843. A stone set into the wall above the hotel porch says 'Rebuilt 1868' and the building to its left dates from 1900. Older photographs show that the wing on the right-hand side of the hotel used to be single-storey and the change in the stonework can be clearly seen in this picture. The porch with the old-style AA sign above the doorway is also a later addition but inside the porch is the original entrance with the name of the hotel set in coloured mosaic in the floor. Reflecting a more leisurely age, an 1898 advertisement for the hotel mentions that parties could be boarded by the week or by the month and it also offered 'posting with steady horses and experienced drivers'.

The Scottish Episcopal Church of St Modoc, built in 1878, is a comparatively small building with seating for 120 people. Prior to the church being built, the congregation held their services in an even smaller building in Graham Street; its manse was accessed by a carriageway from George Street, immediately opposite Bank Street, but this was all swept away when the present Rosebank House in Graham Street was enclosed with a high stone wall. At the time the first church was built there was a statutory limit on the number of persons who were allowed to attend an Episcopalian church so the building was constructed on two levels with an open wall, which allowed the clergyman to minister to twice the prescribed number of parishioners allowed at that time! In the background, the building to the left of the parish church with the window in the gable is the former Auld Lichts Church, which was built in Graham Street in 1801 by seceders from the church at Bridge of Teith. It closed in 1871 and has recently been converted into a private house. Today Muir Crescent has replaced the cornfield and the creeper has been removed from the walls of the church. From this position the parish church or the buildings to the left of it can no longer be seen because the trees have grown so tall.

The Muir Hall and the war memorial stand across from the Woodside Hotel on either side of the Stirling to Callander A84 main road. The hall was a gift to the burgh from Sir Arthur Muir, Bart., of Blair Drummond and was completed in 1922. It was used as the Burgh Offices and the Surveyor's Office until the local government reorganisation of 1975; nowadays it is used mainly for children's playgroups, weddings and local meetings. Today, the houses and bungalows of Muir Crescent run along its far side. Sometime around 1919 a makeshift war memorial was constructed at the Mercat Cross but then the Earl of Moray presented a site for a permanent war memorial on the edge of the ancient Wood of Doune. The memorial was dedicated in 1922, the ceremony being presided over by Dr Burn Murdoch of Gartincaber and the memorial being unveiled by General Sir Ian Hamilton. It carries 63 names of men from the parish; apart from one Royal Navy SWO, they were drawn from seventeen army regiments of whom the Black Watch accounted for 30 names. A further eighteen names were added after the Second World War. Both the hall and the memorial were constructed in Auchenheath stone from a quarry in Lanarkshire and were opened within a week of each other.

Down the hill from the war memorial is the bridge over the River Teith which was originally built in 1535, widened in 1866, and had various maintenance works before and since. It was built by Robert Spittal, tailor to Margaret, queen of James IV, after he was refused a crossing by the ferryman because he had mislaid his purse and could not pay. Robert was a very public-spirited man; he is said to have also erected the bridges of Bannockburn and Tullibody at his own expense and in 1530 he founded a hospital in Stirling. His bridge over the Teith seems to have been an act of revenge on the ferryman who, sure enough, very soon went out of business. The ferry itself was located a little way upstream of the bridge, towards the castle. On the parapet of the bridge is a shield with a spread eagle and in its base a large pair of scissors is engraved, together with an inscription to the tailor. In the latest spell of major maintenance and improvement to this ancient bridge the level of the roadway was raised, partly obscuring the inscription.

The United Presbyterian church adjacent to the Bridge of Teith, also seen in the previous photograph, was built in an old quarry opened for the purpose of hewing stone for the bridge. The Congregation of Monteith built its first church on the site in 1743 and followed it in 1832 with the church pictured here, the manse being built in the following year. The church was built on the site of an ancient chapel, which predated the quarry, and it is thought that stones from the old chapel are incorporated into the south-west part of the bridge. In 1929 the United Presbyterian Church united with the Established Church to become the Church of Scotland; this resulted in a surplus of church buildings in the area but this particular church managed to stay open to worshipers until 1948 and was eventually demolished in the early 1960s. The manse still stands and is nowadays a private house; the old church bell now hangs on the wall near the front door. Nearby are the remains of the entrance to the church, the only traces still remaining of the building.

Deanston House was built in 1820 as the home of James Smith, the manager of Deanston Mill. In 1881 it became the home of Sir John Muir who remodelled the building in the Italianate manor style and added the large entrance hall, the three-storey tower, and the conservatory. He had become a partner in the firm of James Finlay & Company in 1861 and, after James Finlay's death in 1883, became the sole owner of the company.

Sir John and Lady Muir occupied Deanston House for many years and the 1901 census lists the inhabitants as 'John Muir (Baronet) aged 71; Margaret Muir (Wife) aged 59; Catherine (Daughter) aged 26; John (Son) aged 24, Mercantile Clerk; Matthew (Son) aged 22, Mercantile Clerk; John (Grandson) aged 8; Butler, Ladies Maid, Nurse, Governess, Footman, Cook, 3 Housemaids, 2 Laundresses, Kitchen Maid, Scullery Maid' – a household of nineteen people. Sir John died in 1903 and Lady Muir in 1929, after which the house was sold and, for a time, became Newstend private school. During the Second World War it was taken over by the army as a local headquarters, but was then restored and in 1944 became a Co-operative convalescent home.

Deanston House didn't remain as a convalescent home for long and it next became the Deanston House Hotel. When this opened it boasted a fine and elegant conservatory, pictured here, which was on the extreme left front of the building and where weddings were often celebrated. In the early 1980s the hotel was put up for sale and in 1984 the house became a nursing home and part of the grounds, which at one time contained a boating lake, were turned into Deanston Gardens, a private housing estate. In July 2006 the house was once again sold and in September the new owners began a refurbishment programme. In January 2007 the house was re-registered under the name 'Manor Hall Care Home'; the conservatory building still exists but is nowadays divided into patients' bedrooms and a social area.

The River Teith rises in the Trossachs and flows through Callander, where it is joined by the River Leny, and onwards past Deanston on its way to join the River Forth three miles north-west of Stirling. It doesn't pass through Doune itself but is joined on either side of the town by the Annet Burn and the Ardoch. The road up to Deanston village leaves the route to Stirling immediately past the Bridge of Teith, and runs alongside the riverbank with Deanston House on the hillside on the left. The buildings are Deanston Mill, which was first established on this site in 1785. In that year John Buchanan, who had been an apprentice of Richard Arkwright in Lancashire, purchased six acres of land for a lint mill beside the Teith and installed his brother Archibald as manager in what became known as the Adelphi Mill. Unfortunately the discipline of industrial working didn't suit the local people and their hostility to changing their way of life contributed to the mill's commercial failure. In 1794 the brothers were declared bankrupt and the property was bought by a Yorkshire Quaker named Benjamin Flounders although a fire in 1796 caused it to close temporarily. In 1806 James Finlay & Co. purchased the mill and James Smith, Archibald Finlay's nephew, was installed as manager at the tender age of seventeen. In its early days the mill had employed a large number of Poor Law children, usually orphans from different parts of the country, and housed them on site, but when James Finlay & Co. took over they built a community along the lines of Robert Owen's social experiment at New Lanark and named it Deanston. Orphaned children were put under the supervision of a respectable female employed by the company, sent to school and brought up to work in the business. In 1862 the mill hit hard times, mainly due to the American Civil War when there was no raw cotton available, but nevertheless the owners continued to pay the whole workforce half-pay and utilised the downtime to increase the educational facilities.

In its lifetime the mill produced a variety of goods including cotton lace, cotton stylised sheets and towelling using Jacquard looms. At one time over 1,000 workers were employed but by 1953 only 300 remained. One of the mill's biggest problems was that it was purely a manufacturing unit without any facilities for finishing off the cloth. Its output had to be sent to its sister mill at Catrine, Ayrshire, for finishing and this combined with competition from cheap imports eventually led to the mill becoming unviable. It closed down in 1965. The Deanston Distillery Co. Ltd purchased the buildings and converted the seven-storey spinning mill into a still and mash house. Three floors were removed to make room for four steam-heated copper stills and a giant mash tun that are capable of distilling three million gallons of alcohol per year. The Jacquard weaving shed became a warehouse and the old weaving shed provided further warehousing and spacious cooperage. The distillery opened in 1966 and released its first single malt in 1971 as 'Old Bannockburn'. In 1972 the business was purchased by Invergordon Distillers who released the first 'Deanston' single malt that same year. The distillery was closed in 1982 but Burn Stewart purchased the property in 1990 and recommenced production in 1991. The business has developed rapidly since then and its latest offering, 'Deanston 30 year old', was released in 2006. This picture shows how the large main buildings, solidly built and mainly of sandstone, looked around the end of the nineteenth century. The main entrance for the workforce can be seen just before the taller building. The four-storey buildings have been demolished and replaced by a newer block but the seven-storey building still stands proudly at the entrance to the village.

Opposite: In 1829 James Finlay & Co. drew up plans for the installation of eight huge water wheels; these were later reduced to four although it is said that the foundations were laid for all eight. Two were ordered from the Manchester firm of Fairburn & Lillie and they began operating on 3 June 1830. The third and fourth wheels, designed by James Smith, were manufactured in the iron foundry at Deanston Mill itself; they began operating in 1832 and 1833 and were named 'Samson' and 'Hercules' respectively; the latter was said at the time to be the largest water wheel in Europe and the second largest in the world. The oldest wheel, seen here, turned for 120 years. Large water pipes carried the water up from the mill lade to overshoot the wheels so as to give the maximum thrust and power. The water wheels stopped turning on 11 November 1949 and were replaced by a hydro-turbine and steam electricity generating plant. The mill's iron foundry itself closed in 1935.

Each pair of wheels drove a main shaft which passed through the adjacent wall into the mill and drove the machinery by a series of smaller linked shafts radiating from it. The statistics of the wheels are impressive: diameter, 36′ 6″; width, 11′; buckets per wheel, 80; nominal horse power per wheel, 75 hp; total horse power, 300; fall, 33′; speed, 2.1 rpm; water required per day, 40–50 million gallons.

Around 1790, soon after the original Adelphi Mill was opened by the Buchanan brothers, William Murdoch of Gartincaber built a row of cottages that housed around 250 workers. He called the houses 'Murdochstown' but they were soon nicknamed 'Cotton Row'. They were all pulled down around 1830. The village's present name of Deanston comes from Walter Drummond who was Dean of Dunblane and took over the feu of the lands from the Haldanes of Lanrick in 1500. Stobie's famous map of 1783 shows that the village was at that time called 'Deans Town'. This photograph shows the view on entering the village. The mills are behind the camera, the school that was opened in 1897 to replace one on the mill premises is on the left, and the bowling green – nowadays closed and converted into extended gardens – can be seen on the right. Its pavilion is now used for storage of gardening equipment and is in a sadly dilapidated condition.

This clock tower stands at the entrance to the village as a memorial to Margaret, Lady Muir, who was the late wife of Sir James Muir and who died in 1929. The tower stands twenty feet tall by four feet square and has a clock face on each side. It is built of red sandstone that had been quarried from Gargunnock in the 1820s with the intention of building a wheel house at the mill and had been lying unused for over a century. The clock was made by Dykes of Glasgow and was electrically powered from the master clock in the mill. The memorial was dedicated at a service on 28 December 1929 for which almost the whole of the village turned out in the rain. The plaque reads, 'In grateful recollection of the memory of Lady Muir of Deanston, born 30th June 1841, died 28th August 1929. Erected by the inhabitants of Deanston village and her friends'. No longer controlled from the mill after it closed, the condition of the clock deteriorated and stopped working, but thanks to the efforts of the Community Action for Deanston group it was restored to full working order in December 2007. The clock tower is nowadays fenced off from the road and is surrounded by a very pleasant children's playground.

The mill buildings dominate the skyline in this Edwardian photograph of the east end of Deanston. In 1811 James Finlay & Co. built these two rows of houses for their workforce. The block on the left was called the First Division and the one on the right the Second Division. The former were built to a higher standard as they were intended for foremen and other supervisory staff. In their early years the Divisions had four levels of accommodation including a basement and an attic and the 1901 census shows that the houses in the First Division often had nine, ten or even twelve occupants to a house whereas the Second Division generally had only three or four persons, rather odd considering the First Division was intended for superior staff. A communal washhouse was built behind the Second Division. The school can be seen at the far end of the Second Division and probably its schoolchildren were brought out to pose for the photographer. The 1844 Statistical Return records a schoolroom on the mill premises capable of holding up to 200 children who were under a single teacher and whose salary was paid by the company. The children attended school between the ages of five and nine, which meant they were usually able to read and write reasonably well before they entered service in the mill. Those employed in the mill between the ages of nine and thirteen were restricted by the Factories Act to working eight hours per day followed by three hours in the schoolroom; there were around 100 such children who were divided into relays of 33 each so that two relays could be working whilst one was attending school. Children between thirteen and sixteen were expected to attend an evening school four days a week. The mill school closed when the new school was built in 1897.

A later photograph of the First and Second Divisions which must have been taken after 1929 because the Lady Muir memorial can be seen in the background. The row of white houses beyond it have since been demolished but one was notable for having been the home of John Grierson (1898–1972) who is credited with having developed the art of the documentary film and who is commemorated through the Grierson Documentary Film Awards which were established in 1972. There used to be a drapery shop at the far end of the Second Division and the post office was in the shop at the nearer end; in the 1990s many of the houses in the street featured in a few episodes of the television series of *Dr Finlay's Casebook*.

The expansion of the mill led to a further three rows of houses being built around 1820 which were known as the Third, Fourth and Fifth Divisions. A second communal washhouse was built to service them. This was the period in which the new lade, the water wheels, the embankment walls along the River Teith, and the new roadways were constructed by the manager of the works, James Smith. Deanston Works Savings Bank was instituted in May 1817 and by 1831 Deanston had three grocers shops and a haberdashery. This picture, looking towards the mill, clearly shows the Second, Third, Fourth and Fifth Divisions with the First Division obscured by the tree on the left. At the further end of the Third Division was the Co-op's shop and bakehouse; traces of it are still visible in the building. Until 1926 Deanston consisted only of these five rows plus two blocks of cottages but in that year twelve semi-detached houses were built to the west of the village and in 1950 a housing scheme of around seventy houses was built by the County Council. The wooden footbridge near the end of the Fifth Division spans the lade which, when this photograph was taken, had been drained for maintenance purposes. The footbridge is still there but is currently closed as being unsafe; a campaign is in progress to have it reinstated.

The lade was a total of 1,608 yards long from its beginning at the river dam to the water wheels in the mill. Originally it passed under the bowling green, the old hall and the schoolhouse, but in 1949 the bottom section of around 100 yards was filled in to give residents larger gardens. This photograph shows the Fifth Division and footbridge from the opposite angle to the previous one. The lade is in full flow and at this point is several feet higher than the River Teith which flows parallel to it and can just be seen in the distance to the right of the path. The path itself continues alongside the lade as far as the river dam.

Local children are gathered on the riverbank to watch the salmon at the ladder, which was specially designed in the 1830s by James Smith to assist the fish in their migratory journey upstream. The location of this picture is almost a mile upstream from the mill, at the end of the lade. The ladder is still intact today but the present-day walker can no longer reach this spot; the author walked just beyond the point where the Annat Burn flowed into the far side of the Teith but was then stopped from walking any further towards the ladder by a high metal fence topped by barbed wire that stretched across the footpath and the adjoining area. So much for free access to the countryside! Apart from salmon, the Teith was once noted for its fine pearls which were often red or pink in colour. The first pearl was recorded here in 1811 but by the end of the nineteenth century pearl fishing was dying out for lack of stock and over-fishing; however they could still be found occasionally up to the 1950s. Mussels have also been fished in the river since 1120.

The hamlet of Buchany lies just before the Annat Burn one and half miles west of Doune on the road to Callander and is situated just before the Burn of Cambus. The hamlet, seen here looking towards Callander, had a corn mill further along the road, beside the Annat Burn. Around 1790 this mill was one of the principal mills in the parish and was part of the Doune estate of the Earl of Moray; nowadays all that remains of it are two stone mill wheels that lie at the end of the road up to the former Doune Lodge coach house. Buchany itself is almost unchanged from this photograph although the road, nowadays the busy A84 tourist route from Stirling to Callander and the Trossachs, is in somewhat better condition. Also, the large house whose gable is in the centre of the picture has been replaced by two modern bungalows.

This cottage at Buchany, which can also be seen on the right of the previous photograph, is named Gartchonzie. Nowadays a private house, the porch and bench have gone and it no longer sells refreshments or offers furnished apartments as advertised on the signs attached to the porch. The Doune Motor Museum, which housed the Earl of Moray's collection of veteran and vintage cars, was located nearby in the Carse of Cambus steadings and was open for around thirty years, eventually closing in 1998. Its buildings are nowadays used by the Scottish Antiques and Arts Centre.

From the main road at Burn of Cambus a driveway runs up to Doune Lodge, the local seat of the Earl of Moray. The house that formerly stood here used to belong to the Edmonstone family of Duntreath and was called Cambuswallace but in 1809 they sold it to Francis, Lord Doune (later tenth Earl of Moray) and in the following year he built the present house, incorporating some of the old one, and changed the name to Doune Lodge. He needed the house because Doune Castle had not been lived in since the early 1700s and was uninhabitable. This photograph shows the house as it was originally built; in 1912 it was harled and painted white and that is the way it has appeared ever since. Between 1932 and 1952 the house was leased to tenants but since then has again become the Earl of Moray's local residence.

Opposite: The Lanrick estate lies a little way to the west of Doune Lodge along the road to Callander and has a long history. The name means 'a clearing in the wood' and it was originally a part of the ancient Earldom of Menteith. There has been a building on the castle site for at least 700 years. Through marriage the estate became the seat of the influential Haldane family of Gleneagles, but their property was confiscated and sold by the government as a punishment for their part in the 1745 Jacobite rebellion. It was purchased by the Wordie family who lived there for some years but in 1776 they sold it to General Sir John Murray who had made his fortune serving with the army in India. He was a MacGregor by birth but had been banned from using that name under an Act of Proscription. After the Act was repealed in 1774 General Murray reverted to his true name and became head of the Clan Gregor. In the 1790s he commissioned the Scottish architect James Gillespie Graham to design a new property around the original tower and named it Clan Gregor Castle. Unfortunately, the family fell into debt and in 1840 the Laird of Lanrick, Sir Euan McGregor, sold the estate to William Jardine MP for £100,000. Jardine was of Jardine Matheson, the famous Hong Kong and China trading company that was founded in 1832 and which is still in business today, and had made his money from the opium trade; he rebuilt the existing house into the splendid example of Scottish Baronial style seen here, complete with crenellated turrets and a grand front entrance. In 1905 Sir Robert Jardine sold the estate to John Stroyan MP, but after the latter's wife died in 1955 the castle was closed and its contents were put up for sale. Stroyan's grandson, Alistair Dickson, inherited the estate in 1982 but the castle had been uninhabited since 1964 and had become a ruin. In 1994 a fire destroyed the roof and winter storms in 2001 made the structure unsafe. After receiving conflicting instructions from Stirling Council, Mr Dickson took matters into his own hands and the end came on 19 February 2002 when a JCB moved in to complete the castle's destruction. Mr Dickson was subsequently fined a nominal £1,000 for breaching building regulations; local public reaction varied from outright condemnation of his action to sympathy for a landowner who was having to bear the cost of maintaining a ruin that he didn't want.

Gartincaber, situated a few miles to the south-west of Doune off the B826 road to Thornhill, used to be the family estate of the ancient Doig family and the name means 'the grove on the hillside'. Young's 1898 guide to Doune says that 'Gartincaber is an old house of considerable size, the residence of John Burn Murdoch, advocate, who has always taken the deepest interest in the welfare of the people. The Gartincaber tower is a well-known landmark, built as a dovecote for the keeper of the house, and is said to mark the centre of Scotland'. The latter statement about the nearby tower, on the other side of the B826, is nowadays taken with the proverbial pinch of salt!

In 1747 two avenues of trees were planted at Gartincaber at right angles to each other. The avenue to the north of the house was of beech and has suffered badly from gales over the years, but the grove of lime trees that was planted to the west of the house has survived in better condition. Pictured here, it is said to be the finest example of its kind in Britain. The avenue is only fifteen feet wide and some of the trees are up to a hundred feet high.

Coldoch estate lies on the southern boundary of the parish, about two miles south of Gartincaber. For many years it was the home of William McNair Snadden who became the Member of Parliament for Kinross and West Perthshire in 1938 in interesting circumstances. This parliamentary seat had been held for the Conservatives since 1923 by Katherine, Duchess of Atholl; because of her support for many causes that were anathema to Neville Chamberlain's Conservative government she had earned the nicknames of 'Red Kitty' and 'The Red Duchess'. Matters came to a head in April 1938 when she opposed the government's policy of appeasement; she was repudiated by her own local party and a by-election was called for 21 December. The Duchess stood as an Independent candidate and both the Liberal and Labour parties declined to field their own candidates because they supported her views. Her only opponent in the by-election was William McNair Snadden who stood on behalf of the Conservative Party and who won with a majority of 1,313 votes, such was the general feeling in favour of the government after the Munich Agreement of September that year. In 1951 William McNair Snadden was appointed Joint Under-Secretary of State for Scotland, a post he held until his retirement from parliament in 1955 when he was created a Baronet. The oldest part of this fine house, which was once called 'Coldochis', was built around 1513. It was a square two-storey house with a large turret staircase on the north side of the east wing. In 1928 the house was redesigned by the Stewart & Paterson architectural practice who turned it around, the turret which had been at the front of the building being incorporated into the rear of the new building. William McNair Snadden died in 1959 and the house did not survive him for long, being demolished sometime around 1965.

Eastwards of Coldoch is Blair Drummond estate, which lies on the south bank of the Teith. The original house was designed by Alexander McGill for George Drummond, the sixth Laird, and was completed in 1717. Its successor, pictured here, was designed by James Campbell Walker and built nearby in 1868 for Sir George Stirling-Home-Drummond. On its completion the old house was demolished and the present-day safari park's giraffe enclosure has been built on its site. The mansion house, which is in the Scottish Baronial style, stands in the middle of a beautiful park which is studded with large trees and once had formal gardens that were laid out in the Dutch style. Within the grounds is a monument erected to one of the estate's earliest owners, Henry Home, Lord Kames (1697–1782); he became a law lord as well as being one of the leading figures in the Scottish Enlightenment and a pioneer in agricultural improvements. He cleared his estate of around 1,500 acres of moss fourteen feet deep and turned what had been a totally unproductive area into arable farmland. On the death of Lt Colonel Henry Edward Stirling-Home-Drummond in 1912 the estate was put up for sale and was bought by Sir James Kay Muir. On his death he left the estate to his nephew, Sir John Muir (not the Sir John Muir mentioned on page 27). In 1921 the house suffered a bad fire and was rebuilt by James Bow Dunn over the next two years. The present-day safari park in the grounds of the estate was opened in 1970 and today is owned and operated by Sir John's son, Jamie Muir. In 1977 the house itself was sold to the Camphill Trust, a charity who operate it under the name of Camphill Blairdrummond as a community for young adults with special needs. This postcard is dated 28/7/1935 and addressed to Miss Whyte, Fruiterers and Confectioners, Port Street, Stirling. On the back, in Lady Muir's handwriting, is a note saying, 'Most grateful thanks for your generous contribution to the Doune sale which was a great success.'

The original Inverdarroch House stood on the higher ground overlooking the mouth of the Teith, a little east of its junction with the Ardoch. In 1858 John Campbell, who made his fortune trading in the Far East, bought the house from the Edmonstone family and he employed the architect David Bryce, an exponent of the French chateau style, to enlarge the building. It was severely damaged by fire in 1879 but was subsequently restored. In 1898 the house was rented to Sir James and Lady Thompson who lived there until 1902. Sir James had started his career on the Caledonian Railway as a junior clerk in 1848 at the age of thirteen and had risen to become its general manager in 1882 and its chairman in 1901, a position that he held until his death in 1906. He was knighted in Queen Victoria's Diamond Jubilee year of 1897 and was the first railway official in Scotland to receive this honour. During the Second World War the house was taken over by the military authorities who treated it so roughly that, after the war was over, it was reckoned to be beyond restoration. In 1951 it was stripped of its roof and left to the elements and, like Lanrick and Coldoch, it was later completely demolished.